Power of Two

by Dakoda Foxx

BLUE FORGE PRESS
Port Orchard ✸ Washington

POWER OF TWO

Contact:

www.ThePowerTwo.org

(253)257-8067

poweroftwo14@gmail.com

Table of Contents

Power of Two

by Dakoda Foxx

The Start

Power of Two is a 501 (C) 3 non-profit organization that was founded in 2011. Founded by Dakoda Foxx and Jossett Thomas. We started because my daughter has a heart of gold and wanted to do something to help eight youths at her school who was homeless and hungry and needed food and clothing and other stuff.

She made a decision that she would help even if it cost her everything. It almost did. She showed me that it was easy to give help. Not easy to get them places to go to keep warm or some of the necessities that really mattered. So together we took care of them it went from eight to sixteen to thirty-two. We did it and the Power of Two was born.

Power of Two has been helping the community with essential resources and support ever since. We focus on positively impacting youth and families affected by adversities by restoring hope and dignity. We provide food, clothing, hygiene products, household items, cleaning supplies, homeless services, youth programs, women's group, Know your rights training and resources to these communities.

TeamChild

"Stand With Youth"

Thank you to TeamChild and Paul Alig—without them we would not be here.

TeamChild provides free legal services and advocacy for youth involved in the juvenile justice system, child welfare, education, and mental health systems in Washington State. By helping youth secure housing, stay in school, and access community-based services, TeamChild addresses systemic barriers and empowers young people to achieve their goals.

https://www.teamchild.org/
(206) 322-2444
questions@TeamChild.org

King County
625 Andover Park W, Suite 112
Tukwila, WA 98188

Pierce County
949 Market Street, Suite 468
Tacoma, WA 98402

Spokane County
35 W Main Avenue, Suite 316
Spokane, WA 99201

Yakima County
32 North 3rd St, Suite 410
Yakima, WA 98901

Dakoda Foxx

(Dax)

Founder of Power of Two

I have been fighting for youth rights since 2012. I will keep fighting for people's rights till the end. This is my passion and duty.

Helping the elderly, youth, families with hope and dignity. Our program is about love and care in every aspect.

Power of Two Motto

I AM LOVED.

I AM SPECIAL.

I AM WORTHY.

I AM GRATEFUL.

I AM UNIQUE
BECAUSE THERE IS ONLY ONE ME.

18

It doesn't matter how
the donkey got into the ditch,
it matters how it gets out!

You are safe here.

All Races
All Genders
All Sexualities
All Religions
All Abilities
All Ages
All Nationalities
All walks of life

This is a safe place.

Welcome to Power Program 1.0

Power of Two focuses on the professional, economic and character development of inner-city youth and young adults between the ages of 12 and 25 years old from challenging backgrounds. The youth and young adults enrolled in this program come from some of the most challenging neighborhoods.

This program is to help guide you to the point where you can understand where you are and where you are going in life. This will help you find more about yourself and guide on your path to the new you.

Helping youth though transformation and interactive workshops to support youth and young adults in unlocking their full potential 12-part workshop series.

Topics of discussion include:
1. Self-love and value
2. Finding your voice

3. Living by principles
4. Designing your confidence
5. Integrity base decisions
6. Vulnerable You
7. Effective communication
8. Understand your purpose
9. Overcoming adversity
10. Leadership support
11. Money support
12. Advocacy

Our mission is to enhance social and emotional learning through creating fun and interactive spaces for youth, and families to assess their skills and qualities, consider their aims in life and set goals in order to realize and maximize their potential and create unbreakable, healthy bonds while having an impact on their communities at large.

The Power Program 1.0:

This program will inspire, motivate, encourage and enhance the skills they already have and bring out more they didn't know about.

This program consists of 12 Practices in 8 weeks, which will be completed on their own or as a cohort. In addition, an advocate will be available to meet with them in person or virtually on zoom Meetings. They are expected to spend about 2 hours a day participating in each practices for a total of 24 hours of course development.

This enhanced program upon successfully completing the 12 Practices, they will receive a signed Certificate of Completion. Plus, a special gift for all who finish all 12 practices and 8 weeks with all paperwork turned in.

Well we see that youth are impacted in many different ways, so we will do an evaluation of them in stages though out the program. Each youth program is adjusted just for them—no two youth are the same. So growth will be evaluated on the measure of the youth and how far or little their progression is.

Goal 1: The Initial Survey

You are provided with structure, supervision and support from advocates. These advocates work with the youth to create weekly schedules that will help you meet their goals.

This is where you take the time to list what you feel and would like to do after school or work.

Who do they think you can go to for support.?

What do you think is the best thing you have going on now?

What are some changes you would like to make?

These are some of the questions we ask on the survey. Make sure you write these down for later.

Grab a notebook to keep all your answers and thoughts in. This you will need to look back on to help you get through this process.

Goal 2: Your Voice

Finding your voice involves discovering and embracing your unique identity, values, and perspectives, and expressing them authentically.

Individual-based problem solving tools, this is where we listen to what you want and you need. Its geared to help you make decisions about how you want or see the future.

It's a mapping tool we use. That is where you draw out what you think your future would look like. How you would go about getting it. Finding the proper channels to obtain this goal or plan.

This is the start of the week practice:

Shape a personalized journaling ritual that fits your background, your goals, and the kind of voice you're trying to uncover.

1. Write from lived moments rather than from stuff that's coming up. A memory of a family gathering, a song from the past, a scent from your neighborhood. these small thoughts often reveal the deepest truths.

2. Notice what you defend, what you question, and what you long for. Those emotional spikes are clues to your values.

3. Notice when you start writing what you think you should say. That's usually the moment to pause and ask, "What's the truth underneath this?"

4. Allow discomfort. Growth often hides behind the entries you hesitate to write.

5. Treat your journal as a private space for exploration, not performance. Your voice strengthens when it doesn't have to impress anyone.

6. Now use your voice to guide you to the place you want to be.

7. Write down 5 things you feel you notice about how your voice is being brought out.

Goal 3: Attitude and Rethinking

Educated in attitude and Rethinking-based problem solving tools, and specific plans to put the right back in what's been done, including personalized ways for youth to learn new skills/ attitudes to avoid future trouble; allows for easy monitoring and follow up.

How did that make you feel?

What could you have done differently?

Was my altitude warranted?

Instead of getting mad or flying off the handle use the "THINK" model.

T- Think why is this making me mad?

H- How is being mad or upset affecting me and my health?

I- Is this going to matter five years from now?

N- Now you have a choice to stay mad and upset or to do something different.

K- Kick in your boundaries and keep what or who away from you that's causing you hurt, harm or danger.

Calming music activities have the power to change how you interact, learn, and communicates if you get overwhelmed or upset. Music is a great way to debrief and calm down from the outside world issues.

Find music that soothing to your soul. Feel good music will calm you down and some music will heal you too. Music therapy is encouraged.

Goal 4: Relationships

Problem solving tools, Importance of relationships in the family, schools and community, with this model we at Power of Two practice with all our clients. We show compassion and care for each one. We always show everyone is important no matter who, what, or how you are.

We emphasize on relationships because we know all too well we will not get along with everyone we come into contact with. But we teach a better way of how to deal with someone you're working with that's difficult to be around or deal with.

We give the skills that will help you weather there in school or on a job. These skills are very important to maintain a job or in school. These skills won't fix it but make it easier to get the job done and not be too affected by what's going on.

Building strong relationships and building a strong body both require consistency, awareness, and a willingness to grow. When you look at them side by side, the principles almost mirror each other.

Strong Relationship:

People don't need you to be flawless; they need you to be attentive, curious, and emotionally available.

Clear communication is key. Say what you mean, ask for what you need, and listen without preparing your rebuttal.

Boundaries aren't walls they're clarity. Respect Yours and theirs.

Every relationship has friction. What matters is how quickly and sincerely you return to understanding.

Consistency is needed in relationships. Small, steady gestures build trust far more than grand, occasional ones.

Mutual growth for all. The best relationships make room for both people to evolve, not stay frozen in old versions of themselves. You will meet that same person over and over again. You will meet the new version of them. That's evolving.

Strong body:

Start where you are. You don't need to be strong to begin; you get strong by beginning.

Growth comes from gradually increasing challenge and more reps, more weight, more endurance.

Rest and recovery. Muscles grow in the downtime. Pushing nonstop leads to burnout. So rest. You don't have to be on the go all the time. A lazy day watching TV or playing games not going to hurt you for one day.

Moving well matters more than moving fast or heavy.

Consistency beats motivation. A sustainable routine outperforms bursts of inspiration.

Mind your body awareness. Pay attention to how your body responds to tension, fatigue, energy spikes, emotional shifts. You are your first responder to your body notice what's going on and listen to the signs its telling you.

How these two worlds connect you:

This is where it gets interesting—the same habits that strengthen your body strengthen your connections with others.

Relationship Principle

Exercise Principle

Shared Insight

Show up consistently

Train regularly

Reliability builds strength emotional or physical

Communicate openly

Listen to your body

Awareness prevents injury and misunderstanding

Respect boundaries

Respect limits

Pushing too hard too fast breaks things

Repair after conflict

Recover after workouts

Healing is part of growth

Mutual growth

Challenge, when placed well, deepens resilience.

Bringing it together in your life: Treat your relationships like training: intentional, patient, and adaptive. Treat your training like relationships: compassionate, curious, and honest.

Use journaling to track both emotional patterns and physical patterns often reveal each other. Notice where you avoid discomfort. That's usually where the next layer of growth is waiting.

If you want, we can build a simple weekly rhythm that supports both your social life and your life journey so they reinforce each other instead of competing.

Goal 5: Vulnerable You

Positive Behavioral and Supports

Finding support in proactive, prevention and focused work used in school and home life to create predictable, supportive environments. Where you can succeed socially, emotionally, and academically. Instead of reacting to misbehaviors and conflicts that arises. Power of Two teaches expectations, prevention, proactive, reinforces positive actions, and uses love to guide decisions.

Respond to misbehavior with guidance, not shame

Understand patterns

Create predictable, safe environments

Teach what you expect

Reinforce what you want to see

Three Tiers:

Tier 1 – Proactive Supports

1. Expectations are taught explicitly, not assumed. "Ask yourself questions. There's no wrong or right answers here, it's just what you feel and want."

2. Routines and norms are consistent. "Keep going!"

3. Positive behavior is acknowledged regularly. "You're doing good, keep it up!"

4. The goal is to create a climate where you thrive. "What do you do to make this happen?"

Tier 2 – Preventive Supports

1. Small group of friends for those of you who need more structure. Accountability partners.

2. Check-ins, mentoring, social-skills groups are helpful. Join or do one.

3. Increased feedback and monitoring from your close friends and family. These feedbacks are critical to knowing if you're on the right track.

4. The goal is to catch challenges early. Stay on top of the derail train. Get back on track.

Tier 3 - Positive reinforces Supports

1. Individualized plans and behavior assessments to stay on track. "You are the captain of your ship. If it gets off course you're in charge to get it back on.

2. Collaboration with families and specialists. This helps on all aspects of your life.

3. Supports for complex needs. Ask for help when you need extra support!

4. The goal is to help with significant

challenges succeed with hope and dignity. You got this!

Goal 6: Full Opportunities in Community

Problem solving tools, this is where hands on in the community comes into play. Each youth have to do at least one thing in the community for the rest of the remaining weeks.

Pick one person they would like to show a random act of kindness to that week and write a one-page paper why they chose them and why that act.

At the end of the 12-part workshop, look at all the answers and write down what keep coming up in all the things you did. This connects to your interests to you and your community.

You've been thinking about:

1. Finding your voice

2. Building healthy relationships with people in your community

3. Practicing intentional habits that build meaningfully relationships

4. Understanding behavior through intention of others

Power Program 2.0

With the 2.0 program you are working on goals for after school and beyond. We get you thinking about where you're going and how you're going to get there. We lay power tools of knowledge on you.

Goal 1: Career Pathways

What steps could you take to move from where you are to where you could ideally be creating your life?

As we look at the stuff you would like to do, we just pull that out and use that as a base then we go on what something you like to do every day.

Now we find out what you are really good at. This will tell me what type of job you would be best at. We know that we will tend to do a better job at something we love and good at verses something we want instead.

"If we find a job we love to do every day, we will never work another day in life."

We will be using the power module.

Start by reflecting on your interests, passions, and strengths. Identify activities that energize you and make you lose track of time, whether it's writing, fitness, music, or playing games. It's all part of you and it's something that you love.

When you pay attention to the moments when you feel absorbed, curious, or energized, you're basically uncovering the blueprint of what you're built to shine in.

Power Module : Activities that pull you in
1. Tasks where you forget to check the time
2. Things you do even when no one asks or rewards you
3. Topics you naturally research or talk about

These are usually signals of higher motivation the stuff that fuels you rather than drains you.

Strengths that show up without effort:
1. Skills people consistently compliment you on
2. Patterns in what others rely on you for
3. Abilities that feel "easy" to you but hard for others

Those often point toward your natural advantage in life.

Passions that keep resurfacing:
1. Interests you've had since you were younger
2. Hobbies you return to after long breaks
3. Creative or intellectual urges you can't shake

Even if they've evolved, the core themes tend to stay the same.

If you want, we can walk through this together. Tell me one activity that reliably makes you lose track of time, and I'll help you unpack what it reveals about your strengths and direction.

If you have forgotten what your strengths are please refer back to your notebook with your strength and weaknesses.

Let's unpack your roles that align with your passions. For example, a love for fitness could lead to personal training, wellness coaching, or social media management for gyms. If you enjoy creative work like video editing or writing, consider roles in media, marketing, or content creation. Don't limit yourself to one "true calling" as many people find fulfillment in multiple career paths over time.

My friend Chris, he is a DJ and also a radio talk show host. He also does web design and makes videos. He found some things he loves. He said he loved it when he was a young boy. It carries on to his adult life. He loves what he does and he does what he loves.

My former student whose parents wanted him to become a doctor like his dad... Well, the young man loved to draw. He got into trouble in school because he drew on everything. He woke up drawing and went to bed drawing something. This is what he loved to do. His parents insisted that he go to medical school but he wasn't interested. He took drawing in school and was so good.

He came to my program we had option he was like I love to draw and paint. I told him let's see what you can do. He was good. I was impressed with that I asked him what do you want to do after school he wanted to draw and paint. His goal was to paint a mural of himself on a building. Well he graduated and became an artist who has his own studio. And didn't go to medical school. He painted the outside of my building with his mural of himself as a baby. Now he paints many murals all over the state.

This is just a few examples of people who followed their hearts and love for something.

Sometimes your goals don't look like what you had planned.

Here is an example that I learned all too well. My family has few things you can be and they get mad if you don't follow one or all. My family is made of many lawyers, police officers, preachers, nurses. Now I grew up with the punishment of law but wasn't into nursing. But didn't became a preacher or police officer either. None of those things I wanted to do. I loved law with all my heart but I love chemicals more. Okay, okay, now you want to know how all this plays a part in what I am saying.

Well, I went to law school dropped out,

worked at a nursing home training to become a CNA. Nope, didn't like that either. I never forgotten about my love of chemicals so I became a chemical engineer. But I keep coming back to law. It's something that I was good at. And my uncle knew that. I went to for paralegal, yup, became the paralegal. So now I am a paralegal that love chemicals and that use all often but I would say multi-tasking with my loves. That lead me to what I do now. It complements it all.

This all lead me to the part where I use each part of what I learned from them in what I do today. So sometimes that things you love can simply be leading you into what you're looking to do. Keep going till you find the right fit for you.

Goal 2: Leadership Support

Problem solving tools, leadership is important we make sure each you have support in this area.

1. Communication ...
2. Creativity ...
3. Motivation ...
4. Positivity ...
5. Feedback ...

Then we take it to another level by the tool they should have by the end of this program to be a great leader.

1. Integrity.

2. Ability to delegate.

3. Communication.

4. Self-awareness.

5. Gratitude.

6. Learning agility.

7. Influence.

8. Empathy.

Goal 3: Field Support

Now it's time to get out there and see what you learned. Youth and young adults that are of age to go on a job interview will practice and go over things that will make them a successful in an interview. Practice with parents or friends.

We will do a mock interview with a local company that will rate the youth on their skills they have learned. ***This is for the in-person program only.***

Ask yourself these questions:

1. Name your strengths with specificity during this process?

2. What part of this went well for you?

3. What did you learn about yourself?

4. Where did you show leadership today?

Thinking about your own promotion or confidence:

1. Track your wins.

2. Speak your strengths out loud.

3. Advocate for your needs with clarity and consistency.

4. Build habits that reinforce your identity.

You've already been exploring these themes. Finding your voice, advocating for yourself, building intentional relationships you have done so you're not starting from scratch. You're refining them here.

This mirrors the journaling and introspection work.

Goal 4: Money Support

This tool is one of the most important thing to any youth coming through this program. This is where they learn how to balance their books and bank accounts. They will learn money etiquettes.

Manage Money
Understanding Needs vs. Wants
Distinguishing Essentials from Extras
Saving a Portion of Every Dollar
Building Strong Habits that Carry into Adulthood
Tracking Spending
Opening and Using a Bank Account
Setting Short- and Long-Term Goals
Building Credit Safely

Whether through an app, notebook, or bank statements, tracking money helps you see patterns and make adjustments. This is one of the most foundational skills for financial independence.

Learning how checking and savings accounts work, debit cards, deposits, overdrafts, and online banking builds confidence and reduces fear around financial systems.

Youth who set goals (new shoes, a car, college, emergency fund) are more motivated to save and less likely to spend impulsively.

Older teens can learn:

1. How credit scores work
2. How to use a secured card responsibly
3. How to avoid debt traps

Our hands-on building tools:

1. Give them a small budget to manage for an event or project
2. Let them practice comparing prices
3. Have them track spending for one week
4. Budgeting apps designed for teens "it really works"
5. Envelope systems
6. Bank youth accounts
7. FDIC Money Smart curriculum (free and age-appropriate) "this I have found kids are fascinating with".
8. You earned $50—how would you divide it between saving, spending, and giving?"
9. You want a new phone. What's your plan to

save for it?"

    10. This is my favorite one for my gamers: "How would you save for that $200 game or item in the game?"

    Game costs $200

    —>$50 a week for 4 weeks will give you $200

OR

    —>$25 a week for 8 weeks will give you $200

    Saving for a rainy day

    This is a cheat sheet for you to go on. No matter how small you save can lead to big wins.

How much	Months saved	Total 1 year	Total in 5 years
$5	12	$60	$300
$10	12	$120	$600
$20	12	$240	$1200
$50	12	$600	$3000
$100	12	$1200	$6000

Simple Youth Budget: $400/Month Income:

    Save First (25%)$100

        —>Long-term savings/investing $60

        —>Goal savings (car, college, etc.) $40

    Regular Expenses (25%)$100

        —>Phone bill $40

        —>Gas/transportation $60

    Spending Money (50%)$200

        —>Entertainment, clothes, food with friends $200

Building Your First Emergency Fund:

Even as a teen, having $500-1,000 saved for emergencies matters. Your phone breaks, you need car repairs, unexpected expenses come up.

Target: $500

Timeline: 4 months

Weekly savings: $32

4 months x $32 = $128

$128 x 4 = $512

Once this fund exists, you won't have to borrow from parents or dip into other savings when something goes wrong.

Goal 5: Advocacy

Food for thought: Remember this, you don't have to raise your voice to be heard. Talk with a normal tone and authority. It forces people to listen and give them time to hear just what you have on the table.

Now if someone is cutting you off and over talking you and you still want to get your point across, simply say this conversation has been terminated and be quiet and sit and watch who responds to the very words that you just said. That is the person you will address. For they will give you their undivided attention because they want to know why you cut them off. Before they say anything else you have two minutes to say all you needed to say.

Then say no more.

This is a tactile I learned in running for presidency race. It works like a charm in my most everyday life. My practice is to never raise my voice above talk voice. Bring your opponent to you, by making them lean in to hear you.

Now you're ready to go and improve things.

We have taught you how to advocate for yourselves and others. This is a great tool to use. We use the power models.

The goal is for the you to come through this program and be able to teach someone else what you learned and advocate for them.

1. Clarity:

You can't advocate for what you haven't named. Journaling helps you reveal patterns, needs, and boundaries you might not articulate out loud yet.

2. Consistency:

Just like exercise, small, steady actions build strength. Advocacy becomes easier when it's a habit, not a crisis response.

3. Courage:

Advocacy often requires stepping into discomfort and speaking up, correcting misinformation, or challenging norms. Courage grows with practice.

4. Compassion:

Advocacy without empathy becomes domination. Compassion keeps you grounded in humanity—yours and others.

5. Collaboration:

Advocacy is most powerful when it's shared. Invite others into the process, especially the people directly affected.

Advocate for Yourself

1. Use "I" statements to express needs without blame

2. Set boundaries early instead of waiting until resentment builds

3. Ask clarifying questions when expectations are unclear

4. Document your thoughts, patterns, and experiences so you can speak with confidence

5. Practice saying small truths out loud with your voice

Advocate for Others:

1. Speak up when someone is being dismissed or misunderstood

2. Redirect conversations to include quieter voices

3. Share resources, opportunities, or information

4. Model respectful communication and boundary-setting

5. Check in privately: "How can I support you right now?"

Goal 6: Explore opportunities available for them

Now you will show what you have learned by writing one last paper. Then there will be an assessment by your advocates on your progress.

Participants will leave this program with the knowledge, skills, and resources to implement what is learned and also to teach others about what you have learned, in that area of learning focused on implementing better practices to use at school, home and in your community. This is in an effort to create a culture of care throughout your lives.

Power of Two Program

Welcome to the start of the new you.

Each step is going to bring you closer to you and help you on your journey. Not all tools here will apply to you so with that said please take the meat of it and spit out the bones that you can't use.

At first this may seem like a lot or even heart breaking but once you take a look at this you will realize your Power ... This will be hard to take a look at these things but at the end you will see how they all play a role in your life. You will see what needs to be changed, tweaked or removed in your life.

Trying to change yourself, who you are will inevitably lead you to fail and feel hopeless. But if you instead focus on changing your actions without worrying about how it changes you as a person, real change becomes much simpler.

You can't change yourself, so don't even try. I

know that's not what the infomercials and self-help seminars tell you. But forget that. They're wrong. You can't change. Like a thirsty man in a desert chasing a mirage, or a woman peering into an empty fridge there's nothing there. So stop chasing it. Go do something else instead.

Technically, you are both always changing and never changing. It just depends on how you look at it. What you decide is change or not is an imaginary line drawn in your head.

I did a lot of that when I was trying to stop drinking. I gave myself false hope and starts. Had a lot of hard fails. During the times I was trying my mind and actions was dying. I was chasing that mirage and couldn't find the end of the tunnels. I thought failure was all I could do. But when I look back on it I was caught up in that ideal self-involved cycle. What I mean by that is that who I was a person I placed on who I wanted to be. That ideal was tied to my identity my identity was tied to myself. Were we getting any farther than we were before? No.

WHAT IS CHANGE?

When people lay around whining to their therapists and mate's that they're finally going to "change" themselves, they are promising something imaginary and made up. If they used to lie and now they stopped lying, have they "changed"? Are they permanently and irrevocably "fixed"? Will they never lie again? And even if they don't, will it matter? Please tell the hundreds of pissed off mates would like to know.

We don't know what change is because we don't know what the heck we are. If I wake up tomorrow and do the exact opposite of everything I do today, am I a changed person? Or am I simply the same person who decided to try something different?

Here's the problem with using the word "change:" it gets your ideal self-involved. And when you get your ideal self-involved, you become really emotionally attached to imaginary things. You throw fits and beat yourself up and blame others and decide that you are failing badly. But are you?

It's one thing to say, "I want to start going to

the gym every week." It's another to say, "It's time I finally change and become the type of person who goes to the gym each week."

The first statement is simple. You want to go to the gym. So, you go (or not).

The second statement implies that to go to the gym, you must completely reinvent yourself. And that raises the emotional stakes massively. If you succeed (spoiler: you won't), you'll gain this blissful feeling of being a "new person," which will last until the next time you feel crappy and want to "change" again. If you fail, you'll chastise yourself for your failure.

And that's the problem with getting your ideal self-involved. If/when you fail at something, you start thinking: "Maybe I'm kidding myself. Maybe I'm not one of those gym people. Maybe this just isn't me. So why even try?" Because you've decided these arbitrary actions represent the totality of who you are, you will view your failure to get off your butt and put on yoga pants as humanity on your value as a human being. You will hate yourself. And you will be less motivated to "change" or do anything else in the future.

On the flip side, if you succeed, like all drugs, you'll get this nice high and momentarily escape your sense of yourself. But soon, that high will wear off, and you'll need to define for yourself a new type of "change" to accomplish, and you'll pursue that. You'll then become addicted to personal change the same way Eric Clapton was addicted to cocaine or Edgar Allan Poe was addicted to drinking until he passed out face-down in a ditch.

Instead, think of your life merely as a long sequence of actions and decisions. If you're like most people, many of these actions and decisions are sub-optimal. And what most of us mean when we say we'd like to "change" ourselves is simply that we'd like to make slightly more optimal actions and decisions.

For years, I hated mornings. Pretty much my entire life, I woke up late. This would cause a little snowball in my life. I'd be behind on work all day. So then I'd have to stay up half the night working. Then I'd be tired and stressed out the next day. So I'd stay up even later the next night trying to catch up. By the end of the week, I'd be a wreck. Then I thought that I was a night owl. Turns out that I did my best thinking at night but paid for it during the day time.

I still somehow managed to build a career. Don't ask me how. But instead of recognizing that I did okay despite my own bad habits, I made it about me. I made it part of who I was. I decided it was my identity. I said, "Yeah, I'm a good. Forget waking up early. Forget getting sleep. I don't need that. Look at me, I can work all night!"

And you can get away with that when you're 22. But you can't when you're 48.

In my 40s, I began to struggle with productivity. And instead of recognizing my terrible habits, I told myself, "Well, I'm just not a morning person." "Oh, I don't do that sort of morning routine stuff." Without me realizing it, this was so much of me giving up before I started. The times I'd try to get up early or to workout first thing or to eat a healthy breakfast, I'd struggle and immediately tell myself, "See? This morning stuff isn't for me."

Eventually, I had to get over myself. I had to decide that, you know what, I don't know who the heck I am or what I'm doing, but I do know that historically anyone knows, that waking up early and starting the day off with a nice, simple routine is a healthy and productive way to live one's life. Look at Steve Jobs and Bill Gates.

But ask yourself what you got out of getting up early. Is it you got everything done early and the rest of the day is yours to do what you want to do?

And so I did it. I removed my identity from it and just did it because it's a good thing to do. Now I get up early. And I meditate and eat something healthy and go to work.

And does that make me a "morning person?" Does that make me a "productive person?" Who knows? And it was by not caring that made it possible for me to do it.

Keep your "self" out of your decisions, because most likely, it's not about "you." Simply ask yourself, "Is this a good thing to do?" Yes? Then go do it.

Oh, you failed to do it? Is it still a good thing to do? Yes? Then go do it again. And if, at any point, you realize that it wasn't as good as you thought, then don't do it again.

End of story.

CHANGE YOUR ACTIONS, NOT YOURSELF

Most of us who feel stuck in certain habits are stuck because we're emotionally embedded in unhealthy behaviors. A smoker doesn't just smoke cigarettes. They develop a whole routine around smoking. It alters their social life, their eating and sleeping habits, how they see themselves and others. They become "the smoker" to their friends and family. They develop a relationship with cigarettes the same way you and I develop a relationship with a pet or a favorite food.

When someone decides to "change" themselves and quit smoking, they are essentially attempting to "change" their entire routine, the relationships, habits, and assumptions that have gone into many years of doing a singular thing. No wonder they fail.

The trick to quitting smoking "or to changing

the habit" is to recognize that your feel good routine that you have in your mind and labeled "happy" doesn't actually exist. It is just a habit. And it can be raised or dropped at will. You are not a smoker. You are a person who chooses to smoke. You are not a night person. You are a person who chooses to be active at night and sleep through the morning. You are not unproductive. You are a person who currently chooses to do things that do not feel useful. You are not unlovable. You are a person who currently feels unloved.

And changing these actions is as simple as… changing your actions. One action at a time. Forget labeling it. Forget social accountability (in fact, research has found that sharing goals with others can often backfire). Forget making a big rawww about who you are or what you are or what the people thinks about you. The key is to change your routines.

A goal for you to look forward to when you get to program 3 this will keep you going till then…

WHAT DOES CHANGE LOOK LIKE IN YOUR LIFE?

*"Look in the mirror every morning
and tell yourself you love you."*

I've written three ideas that heavily influenced my life, and that I believe can influence your life too.

Now go start the program on next page

Power Program©

Program 1.0

This program was made because of a time in my life I needed these tools to survive. Now this is a daily practice for me and I hope this practice help someone make the changes they need to make in their life.

Each step is going to bring you closer to you and help you on your journey. Not all tool the tools here will apply to you so with that said please take the meat of it and spit out the bones that you can't use.

At first this may seem like a lot but once you apply this to your everyday life it will become second nature to you and you want even realize that your Powering up…

There are three steps to making change happen in your life:

1. Awareness of what needs to be changed

2. Inspiration to change

3. Commitment to change

Don't forget to love on yourself thought the change...

Change your mind for a better life.

"You will never change your life until you change something you do daily. The secret is found in your daily routine."

First start with these steps...

Retrain your mind to start your day:

1. Wake up every morning place your feet on the floor and sit for a few minutes and breath in the morning of waking up.

2. Don't touch your cell phone or computer for an hour after waking up. Whatever it is if it's not an emergency can wait. Take this time for you.

3. Ask yourself as you brush your teeth or getting dressed. List 3 things of what your grateful for today. Say, "I will have a great day!"

4. Now this is important one. One hours before bed don't look at your phone or social media. Now say to yourself what made you happy today and why. Now ask yourself what can you do better

tomorrow. Who life I can make better with a small act.

Remember you are only competing with yourself to do better than you did yesterday for tomorrow.

Do this for 30 days and if it works for you continue on.

Cut out one bad habit:

Pick one bad habit that negatively impacts you and holds you back from who you want to be. Unravel your identity with that habit, and then choose a new identity that doesn't include that habit.

Try these Power ways to change your life and incorporate them into your daily routine:

1. Take full responsibility for your life
2. Prioritize & do the most important tasks first
3. Create your own morning routine (still no electronics for an hour)
4. Daily meditation or mindfulness practice
5. Make health & exercise a priority (15 to 30 minutes a day)
6. Read & learn continuously (you're always a student ready to learn)
7. Discipline & self-control (even if you're really mad sometime the best reaction is NO reaction at all)

8. Consistency (keep going even if you don't see any results. The reward will come if you keep doing it… "Dory says: Just keep swimming!")

9. Follow through with what you say

10. Persistence & perseverance

11. Not afraid to fail (try again failure is not an option as long as you gave it your all. Then it's not a fail it's a lesion)

12. Hone in on your craft daily & sharpen your sword (give it your all)

13. Self-awareness

14. Gratitude

15. Have a support system (your team)

16. Surround yourself with like-minded achievers

17. Goal-oriented

18. Manage your emotions

19. Communicate clearly

20. Value alone time (this is your time to shine with you)

21. Love the journey more than the results (it's on the journey where you will learn who you truly are)

You are going to birth who you are after doing these things for 30 days…

List 10 things you do every day:

1. ______________________________

2. ______________________________

3. ______________________________

4. ______________________________

5. ______________________________

6. ______________________________

7. ______________________________

8. ______________________________

9. ______________________________

10. ______________________________

Power Program©

Program 2.0

Each step is going to bring you closer to you and help you on your journey. Not all tools here will apply to you so with that said please take the meat of it and spit out the bones that you can't use.

At first this may seem like a lot or even heart breaking but once you take a look at this you will realize your Power... This will be hard to take a look at these things but at the end you will see how they all play a role in your life. You will see what needs to be changed, tweaked or removed in your life.

This part is the most emotional piece than the first program you did. When your done hopefully you will find the things that will help you move forward with your life. Remember when you see yourself differently. You start to describe yourself differently as well.

Sometimes trouble is knocking at your door. Standing tall like a tree. It starts off as a little seed, just a little offense, no big deal. If you ignore it, let it go, nothing will come of it. But if you start thinking about it, thinking of how you can get them back, now that little seed is taking root. It's starting to grow, and before long, it will contaminate other areas of your life.

There is no room for problems coming up and causes trouble and many become contaminated by it. You don't see a roots. It's underground; it's hidden. But here's the problem: a contaminated root doesn't grow a good tree. If you have a root of bad it's going to contaminate your life. Here we start by going back and see what has contaminated our life and plant new seeds and grow better roots from today forward.

Remember to keep a notebook of all you write down from now own. This will be used throughout the program and used at the end for program 12…

Let's begin!

There are some things to look at in your life first:

1. What issues or behaviors do you have now?

2. How you react to problems or issues when they come up. Make a list of those things.

3. Major issues you had or having now. Make a list of things and changes, the actions, behaviors that you do now because of this.

4. What relationships that you have now that

you should maybe let go because your formed attachments to the hurt. "Every time you're with this person your always in trouble"?

5. Do you see a pattern to your behavior and the people you have in your life that resembles your issues or problems?

Don't forget to love on yourself thought the change...

Change your mind for a better life.

Choosing your team:

(You have to trust someone...)

1. Chose that person you can trust with who you really are, honest and true, and be friends.

2. These people are with you no matter what. In your ups and downs.

3. Your people are the ones who has your back when you're not around.

4. Your team is your biggest fans and support system. Normally they are two to five people...

The reason you get tired of being around people is because your putting on, because you can't be yourself. **Those are not your team.**

Be selective with who you invest your time in. Wasted time is worse than wasted money...

Distance yourself from people who:
1. Lie to you
2. Disrespect you
3. Use you
4. Put you down
5. Don't inspire you
6. Don't support your dreams or goals
7. Don't celebrate you
8. Most important one don't help you be the best version of you

Negative thinking:
When a negative thought enters your head think positive ones in its place. Positive flip your mind.

Affirmation:
1. I am ready to accept and receive miracles beyond what I have ever experienced

2. When something good happens travel to celebrate. When something bad happen travel to forget. If nothing happens then travel to make something happen.

3. I am giving you permission to root for yourself and while you're at it root for those around you too.

4. We do not need magic to transform our world. we carry all the power we need inside ourselves already.

5. I am the greatest. I said that before I knew I was.

Choosing your team:
Your team is your biggest fans and support system. Normally they are two to five people...

1. ________________________

2. ________________________

3. ________________________

4. ________________________

5. ________________________

"You can master change rather than allowing it to master you."

Power Program©

Program 3.0

Now you should see that you are being pushed out of your comfort zone and things are shifting in your life. Everything that is not going to fit into your new direction is falling by the wayside. Don't try to hold on to something that don't fit you anymore. You wouldn't hold on to a shirt that was two sizes too small because you want to ware it. You would look a little funny with a shirt that was way too small. And who is going to help you out of it. So the same thing for people places and things. Let it go.

This is your break out power season. Sometimes you have to flee your comfort zone to elevate to where you want to go. Sometime its simple as self-care that will make a difference. The closer you get to where you're going the more you lose to gain what you need.

So now reach for those goals and dreams. The ones you may have put on the shelf or corner. Go get them make them a reality. Reach higher than you ever have before. Rise above anything people or situations that could hold you back. Now is the time to follow your truth with in you.

"NOW GO."

The only way to go and be successful is to forgive the people, place and things that held you back no matter what happen it is not your story any longer. It was your past not your future so doesn't hold on to something that will weigh you down and you may look like you're going somewhere but the weight is too great to carry and move.

Now all you have to do is become what you already are…

Forgiveness:

Don't forget to forgive yourself …

Don't stay angry at someone too long. Forgive and move on. You can be hurt by someone that was sent to tare you down that later you find out that it was to rebuild you.

See, you have to have the ability to bend in the moment to receive what is to come. Someone who was a curse at one stage of your life could later down the road be a blessing at another stage of your life.

No one said you had to forget or let that

person re hurt you again but you never know that very person may one day come back around and be the very person that will bless you. So forgive not forget. Keep them at arm's reach and you don't have to deal with them.

You can't stay angry at your enemy's. Because they are your enemy's at this stage but could be your footstool in the next stage and you got to be ready for the change to come. Forgive them and move on.

Remember forgiveness is for you not them and to move forward and succeed. You have to let go and forgive what's not working.

Cut out one bad habit:

Pick one bad habit that negatively impacts you and holds you back from who you want to be. Unravel your identity with that habit, and then choose a new identity that doesn't include that habit.

Try these Power ways to change your life and incorporate them into your daily routine:

1. Take full responsibility for their life

2. Prioritize & do the most important tasks first

3. Create your own morning routine (still no electronics for an hour)

4. Daily meditation or mindfulness practice

5. Make health & exercise a priority (15 to 30

minutes a day)

6. Read & learn continuously (you're always a student ready to learn)

7. Discipline & self-control (even if you're really mad sometime the best reaction is no reaction at all)

8. Consistency (keep going even if you don't see any results. The reward will come if you keep doing it… "Dorie says just keep swimming")

9. Follow through with what you say

10. Persistence & perseverance

11. Not afraid to fail (try again failure is not an option as long as you gave it your all. Then it's not a fail it's a lesion)

12. Hone in on your craft daily & sharpen your sword (give it your all)

13. Self-awareness

14. Gratitude

15. Have a support system (your team)

16. Surround themselves with like-minded achievers

17. Goal-oriented

18. Manage your emotions

19. Communicate clearly

20. Value alone time (this is your time to shine with you)

21. Love the journey more than the results (it's on the journey where you will learn who you truly are)

You are going to birth who you are after doing these things for 30 days…

This part shows you the negative impacts you have picked up along the way from your past. Unraveling your past to make way for the future. This part your gonna need a note book for. You will do lots of writing and analyzing.

Questions to ask yourself:

1. Do I like myself right now with who I am in this moment?

2. What do I really want from my life?

3. What brings me peace in my life?

4. What part of my personality do I need to change or fix?

5. How would I describe a perfect day?

6. What are three things I am grateful for?

7. When was the last time I truly laughed?

8. What's standing in the way of my dreams?

9. The day that I would live over and over again?

10. Are you spending enough time doing what brings you joy in your life?

11. What am I hold on to that I need to let go?

12. Would I enjoy watching the movie made of my life?

13. If my life was a movie how would you title it?

14. What do you do that you enjoy doing every day??

15. What are three important lessons to carry in my life for the future?

16. Who among the people I know bring out the best in me?

17. What lesson I learned this week?

List 10 bad habits you do every day:

1. _______________________________

2. _______________________________

3. _______________________________

4. _______________________________

5. _______________________________

6. _______________________________

7. _______________________________

8. _______________________________

9. _______________________________

10. _______________________________

Power Program©

Program 4.0:

Stanking Thanking

Embracing these is as simple as knowing who you are… changing your thinking is the biggest part of all of this. One action at a time and one thought at a time. Get rid of the STANKING THANKING. Open up to new views and do's. Embrace the new you. Sometimes you have to look at it as. Is it working "MY" way or do I need to get a new "WAY" of doing things.

I sat for a long time on this one because for a long time I did things my way and it wasn't work. I have always been this way take it or leave it. This is me and who I am. But realized that the way I was really wasn't getting me anywhere.

I had to embrace that I was a drunk. I had to realize that I was a hot head and didn't listen to anyone. Thought that I knew it all and I was young and invincible. But I didn't take in account that there is always someone bigger and badder and bolder than you are. I was knocked down but not out. Then I was told try it a different way.

I realize that's a little late in the game. That I should have tried it a different way. I had to take a hard look in the mirror and say you have to change. If you don't you will end up in one of two places. Dead or in jail. So I cleaned up my act and found peace. Peace didn't really look appealing to me at first I thought I was gona die from the boredom. But when I realized that this is what I needed to get grounded. I was ok. Once I took a piece of home and brought it with me. I found that peace all along. It was something I went to everyday and it was my peace all along. Now I bring it into every home and office I am at. I bring the peace and embrace it everywhere I go. My strength was there too... You just got to fine yours...

People who know their strengths and use them often tend to have more success in in many areas. They feel happier and accomplish their goals faster. it's important to have a clear idea of what your strengths are and how you can be used them. Some of your greatest strengths might be easy to recognize, while others go unnoticed because they feel ordinary to you. This part of the program you will identify your strengths and ways in which you are

Power of Two

already using them. You will explore new ways to use your strengths.

Wisdom	Enthusiasm
Artistic Ability	Logic
Optimism	Fairness
Forgiveness	Adventurousness
Independence	Honesty
Open Minded	Assertiveness
Spirituality	Bravery
Self-Control	Intelligence
Social	Athleticism
Creativity	Modesty
Confidence	Empathy
Discipline	Curiosity
Gratitude	__________
Ambition	__________
Flexibility	__________
Common Sense	__________
Patience	__________
Kindness	__________
Awareness	__________
Cooperation	__________
Leadership	__________
Learning	__________
Persistence	__________
Humor	__________

Circle your strengths from the choices below, or write your own:
How to Embrace Strengths & Weaknesses:

1)   Most of us tend to either under- or over-estimate our strengths and weaknesses.

2)   Owning our strengths allows us to utilize them to bring passion, purpose, and joy to our lives and to those around us.

3)   In fact, evidence shows that working from one's signature strengths is one of the surest ways to increase joy and happiness in your life

4)   Owning our weaknesses helps us "get real," accept where we are, and discover peace.

5)   Accepting our weaknesses allows us to improve and grow.

6)   Start by making a list of our strengths and weaknesses.

7)   Choose one strength to strengthen and one weakness to improve.

8)   Our strengths and weaknesses change with life's circumstances, and as we choose to grow.

This week you will write down your 10 strengths:

1. _______________________________

2. _______________________________

3. _______________________________

4. _______________________________

5. _______________________________

6. _______________________________

7. _______________________________

8. _______________________________

9. _______________________________

10. _______________________________

This week your will write down your 10 weaknesses:

1. ________________________

2. ________________________

3. ________________________

4. ________________________

5. ________________________

6. ________________________

7. ________________________

8. ________________________

9. ________________________

10. ________________________

What can you work on this week to change the way you look at these list and use them in everyday life?

Strength exploring:

1. List the strength that help you achieve your goals?

2. What new strength did you discover?

3. How can you use a new strength for your goals?

4. Were you surprised of your new strength?

Weakness exploring:

1. List the weakness that blocked you from achieving your goals?

2. What new weakness did you discover?

3. How did your weakness stop you for your everyday life?

4. What can you do to help you get pass this in your life?

Power Program©

Program 5.0: How You Think

The way you make decisions is very important… Take a look at how you make daily choices. This will set the tone for your life. Many of us make decisions on feelings. We often go on how we feel at the moment. Not what is logical of the situation. When you take a step back and use the (Three "W's" and one "H") model. Many of us are quick to jump when there's a problem or conflict with someone. But to use this method will help you gain more clarity on the situation.

I used to be a hot head and went off at a drop of the dime or a penny to be in fact. But when I realized that this was causing me more trouble than I thought I had to make changes. Not only for me but for the people that I loved that I was hurting with my actions and words by lashing out at them.

I didn't want to see it at first but then I had to sit and take a look at what I was doing. Words hurt, actions were the result of what I was feeling. Either way I was hurting someone I love. That cut to the core when I see the effect of this.

You see word can be said so easy but cut so deeply too. The root of the problem was still not dealt with the only thing that was dealt with was I was angry and I found a punching bag to take it out on in human form.

This model had me stopping myself and putting myself in their shoes on how that made them feel. I would say what was the reason I lashed out on them. Where was I going when I said those awful things? Why did it get me so angry and took me out of myself? How can I change my reactions are towards the situation?

I came up with this model cause my words cut someone so deeply that if it was a knife it would had killed them. I seen on their face how it cut them down and I vowed to never do that to anyone ever again.

Now I practice this in my every day. It's not a practice anymore it's a lifestyle that is imbedded in me now.

Just remember your just one decision from the bad one. So make the right decision. Think of new ways to control your anger and emotions.

This is a model that I use often. It has helped me in many aspects of my life. What, where, why and how has saved me a lot of times. I hope it works for you.

1. What – What is the real problem?

2. Where – Where is this decision going and coming from?

3. Why – Why does this decision matter?

4. How – How will these decisions I make affect me and the people around me?

Three ideals that will change your life in seconds:

I've written three ideas that heavily influenced my life, and that I believe can influence your life too.

1) Attitude

2) Hope

3) Control

Attitude:

We can have control over our attitude and the choices we can make. Gratitude a great attitude is essential. With that, one can adapt to nearly anything in life. It is even better than lots of money in the bank.

Take the time to determine what will help you develop and maintain a great attitude. At the end of the day, write down eight things you are grateful for (anything from having a job, food, housing, to being able to hear.)

Sometimes the attitude that you display will make or break certain situations. Example say you're having an argument with your partner. Your partner is yelling and getting upset by the minute. You start yelling also. Then you see this is not getting anywhere. So you decide to lower your voice and take a different approach. Now you change your tone and you relax and your attitude has calm down. Now if you haven't noticed your partner has stop yelling at the top of their lungs and followed suit of your attitude.

See it only took a moment to shift the dynamics of the argument to another level just by adjusting your attitude. Now your partner is following you without them even knowing this is happening.

Hope:

Hope is critical in all healing. Hopelessness is one of the main features of depression. we hope to have control over the experiences which society deems essential to generating self-esteem: love, power, achievement, money, and more. When we think that we have lost hope of attaining these things. We are helpless in controlling them most people slide towards depression.

But when you look at everything with hope. Look at the problem or issues as I can't change this so I will do what I can at the moment to fix it and have the hope that's needed to get a good outcome. You learn that your mind will look at the issue in a new way other than negative. Remember you attract what you feel or say out your mouth. So if you want the issues to be better you think better and have hope that everything will be just fine.

Control:

The unspoken assumption most of us go under is that we should have control over these things, when in reality they are dictated by circumstances and situations outside of our control. If you just think about it: Did you get to where you are in life without parents, friends, or natural circumstance? Is your ability to maintain your function not contingent on all the people around you functioning in a reasonably consistent and reliable manner?

You are the only person that can control you. Anger is part of life but what you do with that in the moment of the issues is all up to you. Sometimes the outcome of the issue is how you control yourself during the issues. If you explode so will the issue. But if you take a calm approach then you will see that the level of the situation has changed. This is all because you now have gained control over the issue instead of it controlling you.

Sometimes we can dictate a circumstance just

by changing our attitude and controlling our emotions. Remember sometimes the person your auguring with mirror your attitude and watch how you control yourself.

Practice these for thirty days and take note on how your life shifts after you done this for just ten days…

Take the time to determine what will help you develop and maintain these. Here are few some have found helpful:

1. Say or do something kind for someone each day "use the power model to log it in to keep track"

2. Before you say something ask yourself: Is this necessary to say, is it kind, what do I want the person to get or feel with what am about to say?

3. Write down your complaints, then throw them away.

4. Ask yourself: Am I speaking hope into my life?

5. Pause. Before you start your car, sit for a moment and decide to take a grateful attitude to your destination

6. Reflect on how hard times have taught you and made you compassionate.

7. Associate with people who are grateful and have self-control those are the people who will have hope.

There are many ways to get back and maintain your health. Be proactive. Use as many of these tools from the tool box as possible and you'll be better for it!

Decision Making Questionnaire:

Please show how often each of the following applies to you by putting the number that you think applies. After you've done the questions, look over them and think about why you chose the answers you did.

1= no, 2=sometimes, 3=yes

1.Do you enjoy making decisions?

2.Do you like to consult with others about a discussion?

3.Do you stick by your decisions?

4.. When you find one option do go with that?

5.Do you remain calm when you have to make decisions very quickly?

6.Do you feel in control of things?

7. Do you change your mind about things?

8.Do you make decisions without considering all of the implications?

10. Do you prefer to avoid making decisions if you can?

11.Do you take the safe option if there is one?

12. When making decisions do you find

yourself favoring first one option then another?

13.Do you plan ahead?

14 Do you find it difficult to think clearly when you have to decide something in a hurry?

15. Do you carry on looking for something better even if you have made a decision?

16. Do you avoid taking advice over decisions?

17.Do you make up your own mind about things regardless of what others think?

18. Do you work out all the pros and cons before making a decision?

19. Do you rely on "gut feelings" when making decisions?

20. In your decision-making, how often are practicalities more important than principles?

"You can't control
what happens to you,
but you can control
how you react to it."

Power Program©
Program 6.0: Supportive Community & Building Community

No matter your age, building a supportive community can be challenging,

If you're thinking to yourself, 'but who can be or should be in my network?'—that's a great question! There is no 'right' way to build your community or formula for a perfect support system. But, in general, you want people who are caring and loving, whom you can trust, and with whom you feel safe opening up to. Examples can include, but are not limited to, friends, family members, a significant other, a mentor, or a peer group.

Benefits of a Supportive Community:

What's the big deal about support systems? Having a support system in your life is linked to multiple positive benefits. These include higher levels of well-being, better coping skills, and a longer, healthier life.

Support systems have also been proven to reduce depression, anxiety, and stress. Last, but not least, having a supportive community by your side increases your sense of belonging. your community can be people who cheer you on and celebrate you when good things happen or life is going well. Plus, one day you'll be thankful you have these people in your life when crap does inevitably hit the fan.

What Can Support Systems Provide?

A Safe Space:

When you're going through something tough, something you're ashamed of, or something that makes you feel utterly broken, you need someone you can share this with. Being vulnerable is so important to processing and healing, but that's hard to do if you don't feel safe opening up to anyone. That's where your support system comes in! People who can be a listening ear, a shoulder to cry on, or an encouraging advice giver to you when you need it most.

Unprompted Check-Ins:

Going through something tough often makes it tough to reach out for help. These are people who deeply care about you and will check in often with you. A lot of times, having someone reach out to you makes it easier for you to share and open up to them. If you've been withdrawn, your support system can check in and help you find a healthy way out.

Positive Encouragement:

Sometimes we just need someone in our life to be positive when our own minds can't quite figure out how to. The people in your life who you can really trust and rely on are those positive, encouraging people. Whether you need someone to remind you that you're loved and cared for, or someone to encourage you to do something that's good for you, your support system can do that. Also, these people are often the ones that inspire you simply by being themselves and living their lives, which can be a big help when you're struggling.

Healthy Distractions:

We've all been there—just needing a distraction from the storms, stress, and struggles of life. While there's nothing wrong with bingeing that new Netflix show or eating a pint of ice cream, those often aren't the healthiest things to continuously do.

When you need a healthy distraction, look no further than your support system. You can watch your favorite movie with them, go for a walk together, or simply give them a call. There are tons of activities and things your support system can help you do to distract yourself in a healthy way and be filled up in the process.

Extra Help:

Struggles often make basic living even more difficult. That's why having a supportive community in your life is so important. Your people can help you with food (bringing you food or groceries, cooking for you, or helping you cook), cleaning, childcare or babysitting, appointments (making appointments, reminding you of upcoming ones, going with you to them), finding professional help, and more. And the thing is, these people who love you so deeply would absolutely love to help you out with whatever you need.

You can use the toolbox as much as you need to get though the program. Just remember that you are in control of your own destination. We are here just to guide you.

The power model is for you to log what you did and how you feel that week. Make sure you log in you will see it all ties in together.

The Power Model

P - Proficient
O - Opportunity
W -Work
E - Encourage
R - Reward

5 Ways to Cultivate a Supportive Community:

1. Determine Who You Want in Your Community

This isn't meant to be a mean, exclusive type of deal. However, figuring out who you want in your corner makes it easier to cultivate your community with said people. A great place to start is making a list of the people who you already interact with in your life, regardless of how close or friendly you are. Think of all the places you go every day—hangouts with friends, work, neighborhood, home, organizations you volunteer at, school, coffee shops, the grocery store, the gym, etc.

Next, ask yourself the following questions, provided by Road to Growth Counseling, about each person you wrote down on your list. Feel free to add your own attributes such as "is this person compassionate and kind?" or "do they make me laugh?" that you feel are important for your support system.

Do I feel respected by this person?

Do I trust this person?

Does this person bring out my best qualities?

Does this person allow me to feel good about myself?

Do I leave interactions feeling positive?

Finally, put a star next to each person who you feel is supportive as characterized by the attributes above. This can be the start of your support system! But don't worry if you have very few people starred. The very fact that you know the type of person and characteristics you want in your community will greatly help you when meeting and connecting with people moving forward. Also, figuring out what you need in a support network, such as someone who can relate to a specific issue or people who live close by that can help you cook or clean, will help you begin to create your supportive community as well.

2. Start with One Person

You don't have to build your whole network overnight. Most people don't. It's completely normal to start with just a few people and let things grow at a pace that feels real. And honestly, that's usually how the best relationships form anyway. It's not about how many people you know it's about the quality of the connections you build. A couple of solid, genuine relationships will carry you a lot farther than a long list of shallow ones.

You don't have to map out your whole community all at once. Start with one person you genuinely trust someone who's shown up for you before. Let them know how much their support means to you, and be honest about wanting to build a stronger circle around yourself. People who care about you usually want to help, and you might be surprised by how willing they are to walk with you as you figure out the rest. They might even have ideas about others who could be part of that circle.

It's also a good reminder that not everyone in your community needs to know or be connected to one another. While it could help to have a few that are connected so they can best come together to help you in some situations, it's also totally okay to have people from different areas of your life all participating in being your support network. Its encouraged to have some people that's not connected.

3. Go Deeper in Your Relationships

You can't expect someone to show up for you if you never let them in. Being supported means being willing to be open, honest, and a little vulnerable and that's tough to do with someone you haven't built much depth with yet. But that's okay. Everyone starts somewhere, and there's no better moment than right now to take that first step. Even a small, honest conversation can be the beginning of a deeper connection.

Building a supportive community is going to require you to grow your relationships with the people in your life. We know it's scary, but it's also so important and will be well worth it. Don't worry if you don't know where to start. Here are a few ideas of ways you can grow deeper in the relationships with the people in your life:

A) Invest more time (if possible).

B) Start hanging out more often or for longer periods of time. This builds a greater connection and allows someone to be involved in more of your life.

C) Be intentional with the time you do have.

We know everyone is so busy these days and investing more time may not always be possible. If that's the case, make sure you're intentional with the time you do have. Share about what's going on in each other's lives and ask deeper questions to get to know each other better.

Communicate well:

Communication is key for your support system. Let someone know that you want to build a deeper foundation. Open up about what things are making that difficult, goals you have for the relationship, or things they could help you with. The better you communicate, the more supportive someone can be.

Practice being vulnerable:

This one is scary, but honestly, the best way to grow deeper is through vulnerability. And the best way to grow more comfortable being vulnerable is to practice opening up to people. Oftentimes, the other person will reciprocate, and you both can build a deeper connection together.

4. Accept Help When Offered:

Many people love the idea of a support system or community but fail to or don't want to actually use it. It's not easy, and we get that. You may think there's not enough time, you don't want to be a burden, or you're better off alone. There may be fear of being awkward or getting rejected. But the truth is, there's really no point in a support system if you're not going to lean on those people for support when you actually need it.

If someone offers help and is turned down once, hopefully, they would continue to ask and offer their support in the future. But, unfortunately, if someone continues to offer help and continues to get turned down, they may (unintentionally) stop asking altogether. Then you might see it as people don't want to help when it's really your fear fueling a self-fulfilling prophecy.

Now, you don't have to say yes to every single thing someone offers to do—especially if it wouldn't actually be helpful for you. If that's the case, let the person know what would actually help. Or tell them that you appreciate their offer, you don't need it at this time, but that you might need it later and to check back in. But, practicing saying yes to help and receiving it from others allows you to actually use and build up your support system.

5. Find a Group that Already Exists:

We understand that creating your own support system can be tough and exhausting. The good news is that sometimes someone has already done the legwork to create a network that could be there to support you. Examples of this are peer-led or support groups, such as grief groups or AA. The benefit of this is that oftentimes people who have gone or are going through similar things as you can better support and be empathetic based on experience. It's also often easier to open up to those who 'get it' and have been there themselves.

A second idea is finding a group or community to join based on a shared passion or interest. This could include things like sports or an exercise class, hobby-based groups or meetups (painting, cooking, writing), musical events, etc. While they may not all have gone through what you are, you can build a bond and connection on shared interest, which then allows you to open up as you grow deeper in your relationship.

6. *BONUS* Be Patient:

Last, but not least, we're giving you a *bonus* tip which honestly may be the hardest of them all. That is: be patient. Developing deeper relationships, practicing being vulnerable, and cultivating a supportive community all takes time. It won't happen overnight; it won't be built in a day. It can be easy to get frustrated or feel lonely, so we want to remind you to give yourself grace and compassion as you figure out this journey. The fact that you are wanting to build a support system already says so much! If you are putting in the effort, it will pay off. Remember to approach the process with patience and compassion for yourself and others.

Wrapping Up:

We hope you can see and understand the importance of cultivating and having a support system in your life. Because the truth is, life is tough. But you don't have to go through any of it alone. When you don't know where to start, simply connecting with one person is enough. That person can help you meet and/or connect with others, and slowly build your support system from there.

If you truly don't feel that you have anyone you can open up to, or if you want some help finding and building your support network, we've got you covered. Power of Two will be there for you. We can connect you with a caring, supportive person who wants to be there for you and help you cultivate a supportive community so that you can flourish and thrive. Go to the link below to get started!
www.Thepowertwo.org

Thank You

Thank you for reading this book. I wrote this book so it could help others. Just like it helped me. My life was transformed by things in this book and I use them still today. What was meant to break me made me a better person. I believe that nothing happens by chance. Every person I met, every door that was closed, every yes that was said, every hurdle I had to endure was all leading me to this place right here.

I was placed here to help many people and to help lead the way for our next generation to take over and lead the way. I pass the torch to them. Somehow I know that we are in good hands. It may not seem like it right now but I know and feel that the buck stops here and begin with new soil. History may just may rewrite itself.

Don't look at this as a goodbye but a gift of

love I leave for the world to follow. Just a glimpse of what was and what will be. Use this tool to carry on. Change and touch the lives of one person at a time.

Love,

Dax (Dakoda Foxx)
and Josie Thomas

"I am not making any noise."